GOD'S
Messages
for a *Wonderful*
Woman...

Inspired by Faith

Wonderful Woman
©Product Concept Mfg., Inc.

Gods Messages for a Wonderful Woman
ISBN 0-9843328-2-0

Published by Product Concept Mfg., Inc.
2175 N. Academy Circle #200, Colorado Springs, CO 80909

©2009 Product Concept Mfg., Inc. All rights reserved

Written and Compiled by Patricia Mitchell
in association with Product Concept Mfg., Inc.

All scripture quotations are from the King James version
of the Bible unless otherwise noted.

GOD'S
Messages
for a Wonderful Woman...

Let these devotions draw you closer to God and His
wondrous, unchanging and unchangeable vision of you.
Let yourself bask in the warmth of His embrace as you
learn how God sees you *through the eyes of love*.

It is not those who commend

themselves that are approved,

but those whom

the Lord commends.

2 Corinthians 10:18 NRSV

Through the Eyes of Love

Some women spend a considerable amount of time in front of the mirror each morning, while others steal a quick glance at themselves before dashing out the door. Perhaps you're somewhere in between. No matter how — or how long — you look at yourself, God looks at you adoringly.

God sees beyond appearance. He looks at who you are with eyes of affection. Because of God's unconditional love for you, you need never worry about being enough, doing enough, or achieving enough to earn His approval. You already have it, and more. See yourself the way God sees you, and see a beloved and beautiful woman.

God, you know me better than I know myself, and you love me.
Let me see myself through the eyes of your love.
Amen.

Carry each other's burdens,

and in this way

you will fulfill

the law of Christ.

Galatians 6:2 NIV

Many Responsibilities

Have you ever taken a good look at your daily to-do list? In all likelihood, you have a full schedule of things you need to do and places you need to be. Sometimes, however, you might feel overwhelmed by it all.

Because people see you handling everything so well, it may not occur to them to ask if they can do anything for you. And it may not be easy for you to admit that you need a break, a rest, and a helping hand from time to time. Take time now to remind yourself that God does not expect you to carry everything alone, but has placed people in your life to ease your burden and help carry the workload.

You are always willing to help others — let others know the blessing of being able to help you.

Lord, when I feel overwhelmed by everything I need to do, let me pause and ask you for your guidance, your direction, and your strength, and bless me with the gift of others willing and able to help me in time of need.
Amen.

My sheep hear my voice,

and I know them,

and they follow me.

John 10:27

Good
Listening

We live in a noisy world! News comes round-the-clock, our friends can reach us at any time, and instant communication is only the click of a mouse away. With all the words and voices swirling around us, however, it can be hard to hear the one important voice – God's.

Take some time out today to experience a restful silence, and in this silence hear the gentle whisper of God speaking to you in your heart. Imagine watching white clouds float across the sky, feeling a gentle breeze caress your face, and listening to tiny songbirds chirp from the branches of swaying trees. In the stillness of these moments, let God renew and refresh your soul.

Today, turn away from the world's distractions and listen to His voice, the all-important voice of God.

Lord God, help me always to hear your voice
among all other voices, and let my thoughts, words,
and actions be attentive to your will and desire for my life.
Amen.

For unto every one that hath

shall be given,

and he shall have

abundance.

Matthew 25:29

Abundance

Most of us have come to realize that happiness in life does not increase in proportion to the number of material things we can accumulate. Indeed, we have come to a point where down–sizing is applauded and saving, rather than spending, is a national trend.

God, however, still deals in abundance. When He gives spiritual gifts, He gives in abundance, and when He blesses, He blesses in abundance. He offers you the depth of His comfort as you turn to Him, and He holds His arms wide open as you bring all your cares, burdens, and anxieties to Him. God's heart remains spacious, and His love continues unchanged through all generations.

As you thank God for your blessings today, open your life to receive even more. The Lord, your God, still believes in abundance.

God of all good gifts, open my heart and mind
to see and appreciate all the ways you have blessed my life so far.
Let me live in thanksgiving for your
abundant blessings each day.
Amen.

For God hath not given us

the spirit of fear;

but of power,

and of love,

and of a sound mind.

2 Timothy 1:7

Rest Easy

At one time or another, all of us have spent a fitful night worried about what the future has in store for ourselves or for our loved ones. After all, we're aware of what's going on around us, and we've lived long enough to know what can happen from one day to the next.

God knows these things, too, and that's why He gives us an antidote to fear. In His Word, God assures us He has provided us with His Spirit of power to use against feelings of fear, and His Spirit of love to overcome the things that cause us to be afraid. In addition, God enables His own to receive spiritual wisdom and understanding, leaving no more room for timidity and fear.

Praise God for the spirit He has given to you, and enjoy a good night's rest every night.

Creator God, thank you for the spirit of power,
love, and wisdom you have given to me.
Keep me always free from fear
and grant me restful nights and peaceful sleep.
Amen.

And we know that all things

work together for good

to them that love God,

to them who are the called

according to his purpose.

Romans 8:28

Why?

When you're going through one of life's rough patches, it's only natural to ask God for an explanation. "If I'm so loved by God, and if I'm such a wonderful woman," you might think to yourself, "then why did He allow this to happen to me?"

Beloved woman of God, never let the unfortunate events of life, the accidents, the disappointments, the failed plans shake your faith and trust in His Love for you. Why it happened to you may never be answered this side of heaven, but God's clear and unequivocal message to you is this: He has the will, the power, and the desire to work things out for your good.

He has also promised to do so.

In the circle of God's comforting arms, receive hope and strength as you watch Him work through all things for your eternal good.

God of my heart, grant me patience and wisdom
in all life's struggles as I learn more and more
about your loving ways with me.
Amen.

Or take ships as an example.

Although they are so large

and are driven by strong winds,

they are steered

by a very small rudder

wherever the pilot wants to go.

James 3:4 NIV

Word Power

Words comfort, curse, heal, wound, lift up, put down, reveal a lie, hide the truth. No one would deny the power of words!

In the Bible, the tongue is compared to the rudder of a ship that, though a small part of the ship, makes the ship head in whatever direction the pilot dictates. In the same way, the tongue — such a tiny member of the human body! — holds astonishing power. The words that the tongue forms can make life better or bitter for others. The things that flow across its surface can help or hinder God's message of love for all people.

No woman is so insignificant that what she says doesn't matter, or so powerful that she can speak without consideration for others. For all of us, our words steer the course of our relationship with others and with God.

God of my heart, fill me with your love
so my words will keep me on course.
Let my tongue express the truth in love, and may my words
work to the good of my family,
friends, and everyone I meet.
Amen.

Carry each other's burdens,

and in this way

you will fulfill

the law of Christ.

Galatians 6:2 NIV

Celebrate!

God's spirit is at work in you, and it shows. Perhaps a sense of modesty keeps you from counting all the kind, caring, and compassionate things you do for others each day, but people realize. Maybe humility prevents you from remembering how many lives you have touched with your helpful, thoughtful ways, but people know. It's true – you do all this and more!

In His message to you today, God invites you to celebrate His Presence in your life, because it's through Him that you have your strength, your power, your happiness. God has done so much through you already, and it's exciting to imagine how much more He will do as you continue to let His Spirit lead you each day.

Today, pause to thank God for the gift of you. Today, celebrate the spirit...celebrate the joy...celebrate you!

Lord God, I am amazed at the power of your spirit.
Help me always to give thanks and praise to you,
because it is only through you that I have my talents,
my confidence, my strength.
Amen.

Be ye therefore

followers of God,

as dear children;

and walk in love.

Ephesians 5:1–2

God's Path

The problems and pressures of daily life threaten to come between us and the path God has set out for us and God's direction for us to walk. In the Bible, however, God gives us His sign posts to keep us centered on His path and focused on His Leadership.

While human nature prompts us to scramble for strategies to overcome our problems, God's Spirit leads us in a different direction. Under the guidance of God's Spirit, we are able to travel not encumbered by fear, but enlightened by love, wisdom, and goodwill. Led in the path of God's Truth, we can step forward in trust, knowing those things vexing us today will work out in God's good time.

When the problems come and the pressure's on, let God keep you on His Path!

Guiding Light, show me your path,
especially when the problems and pressures of my day make me
think I need to solve everything myself.
Keep me firmly on your path of light and truth,
and enable me to walk in love.
Amen.

Give unto the LORD

the glory

due unto his name;

worship the LORD

in the beauty

of holiness.

Psalm 29:2

It's a Beautiful Day

What do you consider beautiful? A brilliant sunset...
a perfect bloom...a summer's day...a scenic landscape...
a magnificent work of art...an emotive song...a warm smile
of friendship...a few whispered words of love.

Beauty embraces thoughts and emotions, lifting our human
spirit high above the mundane elements of our everyday
lives. In the presence of beauty, we feel elated, joyful, glad and
grateful to be alive at this time and in this place. Then, when
things return to normal and we're once again back to our
routine, we see even the most ordinary things in a new light,
the light of beauty.

Right now, call to mind a moment in your life when you
exclaimed, "This is beautiful!" and with those same eyes —
the eyes of beauty — look around you and taste, see, and feel
beauty everywhere.

Lord God, open my eyes to the splendor
of your world and the beauty of everything around me today.
With all my heart I thank you for the privilege
of being here at this time and in this place with you.
Amen.

Open my eyes

that I may see

wonderful things

in your law.

Psalm 119:18 NIV

God's Good Word

From cover to cover, the Bible is God's story of love for you, His beloved woman.

God gave you the Bible for the purpose of revealing Himself and His thoughts to you. Whether you've read and heard certain passages time and again, or the verses are new to your eyes and ears, God has something to tell you, to promise you, even perhaps to challenge you. Though a particular message may seem unclear to you at the time you read it, its meaning will shape and enrich your spirit as the days and years of your life unfold.

Let God speak to you through His story of love, the Bible. Keep the words you read and hear close in thought, in mind, and in heart, and expect to discover even more wonderful things about the wonderful God who loves you.

God Almighty, you have given me the Bible
for my learning and my guide. Keep me always attuned
to the meaning of your words and open my eyes to see
the wonder of your love for me. Give me ears to hear, Lord!
Amen.

And on the seventh day

God ended his work

which he had made;

and he rested

on the seventh day

from all his work

which he had made.

Genesis 2:2

Rest

When we need more time for all the things we need to get done in a day, we cut down on the amount of time we spend in rest and relaxation. Let's face it, we all do it!

God's message for you today talks about the matter of rest. Busy women like you are susceptible to sacrificing your rest time to get a few more things done, to make a few more phone calls, to send just a few more e-mails. While all these activities are happening, however, take a moment to consider what's not happening: your God-given body and soul are aching for rest, for renewal, for restoration.

Never feel guilty about taking time for rest. It's something God wants for you, even – and perhaps especially – on the busiest of days.

Heavenly Father, keep me from getting so busy
that I forget to rest. Remind me, Creator-God,
of the example you have set,
and fill my heart, soul, and body with your peace.
Amen.

O give thanks

unto the LORD;

for he is good.

Psalm 136:1

Thank You

"Thank you" shows your appreciation to someone for a gift or a kindness, and "thank you" is also a gift of gratitude you give yourself.

The same holds true when you say "thank you" to God for the many blessings He gives to you each day. Of course God knows you're grateful for what you have, but He also knows that when you consciously and actively thank Him by naming those blessings, those gifts, you bring to yourself another blessing – the blessing of a heart filled, even brimming over, with genuine gratitude.

Through the words of the Psalmist, God reminds all His children, both big and small, to say thank you to the Giver of all good things, and to say it every day – and give yourself the gift of a grateful heart.

Heavenly Father, thank you for all the blessings
you have showered on me,
and most especially for the blessing of life itself.
Grant me a grateful heart for all the gifts you give me every day.
Amen.

"I am the Lord's servant,"

Mary answered.

"May it be to me

as you have said."

Luke 1:38 NIV

Never Say Never

Throughout the Bible, we read of women chosen by God to do great things, and the most honored among them is Mary, the mother of Jesus. In her teen years, Mary received God's message that she would bear the Savior of the world. Her reply? "I'm your servant, Lord. I'll do whatever you ask."

Mary's trusting reply is one wonderful women like you have said many times, because they give so generously of their time, talents, and skills to others. They know, as you know, that when God gives a job, He also provides the power and the resources to get the job done.

The next time God chooses you for something that at first seems difficult to accomplish, remember Mary's reply. God has given you the power to do great things in the past, and He will give you the same power today and every day in the future.

Lord God, thank you for the ways you have shown your power in my life so far, and grant me the desire to accept in complete faith whatever task, big or small, you may choose to give me now.
Amen.

For I reckon that the sufferings

of this present time

are not worthy to be compared

with the glory

which shall be revealed in us.

Romans 8:18

Pros and Cons

Many of us, when confronted with a difficult decision, make a list of pros and cons. If we feel the pros outweigh the cons, we'll go ahead with our decision.

Sometimes it's helpful to look at life's trials the same way. Make two columns and start a list, first with the cons — those things happening in your life you wish could be different. Then, go to the pros — those things happening in your life that are going well, the joys, the successes, the things that make you smile.

As a child of God, you have something to add to your list of pros that nothing can diminish, and that's God's Love. In any list of yours, the pros will always far outweigh the cons, no matter what's happening in your life right now.

Lord God, thank you for giving me
the assurance of your presence in my life.
There are no difficulties I face
that can diminish the joy of knowing you.
Amen.

God is faithful,

by whom ye were called

unto the fellowship

of his Son Jesus Christ our Lord.

1 Corinthians 1:9

Promise Kept

Most of us, at sometime in our lives, have been the victim of a broken promise. Some wonderful woman was once the hurt friend left behind by a popular girl. Someone has been the stunned wife of an unfaithful husband. Whether the wound has long healed, or the wound is recent and raw, God has a message for you today: I am faithful.

Throughout the Bible, God promised His people He would be faithful to them, and He was — time and time again. Though they turned their backs on Him, God remained faithful. No matter how far away they took themselves, God called them, watched for them, waited for them to return. Regardless of how many times they were faithless, God remained faithful, according to His Promise.

In the midst of changing times and circumstances, God never changes. He is faithful, and you can depend on Him.

Faithful God, your faithfulness allows me
to put myself in your care and protection.
Confident in your promise,
I place my trust in you!
Amen.

For thy word's sake,

and according to thine own heart,

hast thou done

all these great things,

to make thy servant

know them.

2 Samuel 7:21

Just Because

When accidents happen, we might cry in desperation, "Why me?" Some of us, however, are just as likely to use those words when we find ourselves receiving an unexpected blessing. We think we don't deserve it, so we ask, "Why me?"

When you consider God's goodness to you and His work in your life, do you ask, "Why me?" If so, you're not alone. In the Bible, King David uttered those words when he heard God's promises to him. "Who am I that God should bless me this way?" the king cried. God's answer? "Just because." The answer God gave David is the one God gives you.

With open arms, accept and embrace all the ways God chooses to bless you. God will continue to bless you richly — just because.

Good and gracious God,
you have richly blessed me in so many ways.
Grant me the grace to embrace and enjoy
everything you have seen fit to give me.
Amen.

The LORD

will fulfill his purpose

for me;

your love, O LORD,

endures forever.

Psalm 138:8 NIV

A Good Purpose

When our plans are thwarted by one of life's surprises, it's only natural to feel disappointed, even to react in anger because what we wanted to do is no longer possible.

At those times, God would urge us to turn our full attention to His plans, because His Purpose for our life will not be thwarted. In the events that take place, the challenges we face, the reality we deal with every day, God is fulfilling His plans and purpose for us. What plans and what purpose? We may never hear all the details this side of heaven, but He has told us enough. He has told us He has a good and true purpose for each of our lives.

As your life unfolds with its myriad of planned successes and unplanned twists and turns, know that each day life is unfolding according to plan – God's Plans.

God, when I must lay aside my plans,
help me do so with my heart set on your will
and my eyes open to your purpose in my life.
Amen.

Rejoice with them

that do rejoice,

and weep with them

that weep.

Romans 12:15

How to
Greet People

The apostle Paul has this advice: If you meet a friend who's weeping, weep right along with her. If you meet a friend who's happy, then share in her happiness.

When we meet certain people, it's easy for us to fall into the trap of playing a familiar role — the role of advisor, of critic, or judge. It's common to sift what we hear from someone else through the sieve of our own experiences and the perceptions we hold of that person. It's natural to reserve our deepest feelings for things we personally feel are important.

Paul's advice is just as true today as it was the day he wrote it. When you meet your friends today, make a special point to discover if they are weeping or rejoicing, and respond accordingly.

Lord God, when I see my friends today,
help me remember to meet them
where they are and share in their sorrows and joys.
Amen.

Thy word is a lamp

unto my feet,

and a light

unto my path.

Psalm 119:105

Shining Light

Many of life's passages are difficult. Some women recall the transition from childhood to adulthood, from single life to married life, from married life back to single life, or from younger to older as an especially long and difficult struggle.

Whenever the journey gets dark, God gives His people His Word as a guiding light. In the Bible, His people find His messages of love and encouragement to renew their strength, enabling them to take one step at a time, one day at a time, along a new and as yet unexplored path. They hear again His warnings designed to keep them steady and steadily on His path, and they read once more of the women and men of God who have gone before.

When the path gets dark, God's Word shines ever bright. You need never be afraid to take the next step.

Heavenly Father, thank you for giving me
the light of your Word. Grant me the wisdom to find
your will and purpose in all of life's passages
so that I may welcome each with thanksgiving and gladness.
Amen.

He brought me out

into a spacious place;

he rescued me

because he delighted

in me.

Psalm 18:19 NIV

Blessing
on Blessing

When you count your blessings, do you realize why you have so many? It's not because you've earned them (although you have!), or because you deserve them (although you do!).

It's simply because God delights in you!

Human reasoning says we must work to get what we want to receive, but God's reasoning doesn't see it that way. He showers blessing after blessing on us without regard to how many volunteer hours we have put in this month (although He is glad for each one), how many times we have visited a hospitalized friend (although He loves to see this), or how many years we have been a Christian (although He applauds each moment).

Beloved woman, enjoy every single blessing God has put into your life, and rejoice in all the wonderful things you do!

Lord God, thank you for all the blessings you have showered down on me. Let me not look at my blessings as something I must earn, but as a sign of your gracious love and your eternal delight in me. Amen.

I will praise thee,

O LORD,

with my whole heart;

I will shew forth

all thy marvellous works.

Psalm 9:1

Rejoice!

As busy women, we often go from one task to another without stopping to acknowledge everything we have accomplished and to celebrate our victories — those many finished projects, realized goals, and achieved milestones.

Celebrations, however, are necessary, because celebrations not only mark significant and important life events, but serve to remind us how and where God has used and is using our gifts and talents.

God's message for you today encourages you to think of your most recent accomplishments and give thanks to God for the God-given pleasure of being able to plan, do, and complete a task, reach a goal, hit a milestone. Then, why not share your joy with a couple of co-workers, friends, and family members? Tell them what you are celebrating, and invite them to rejoice with you.

Rejoice always in all God's marvelous works through you!

Dear Lord, it is a privilege to do the things
you have given me to do,
and I rejoice in your goodness to me.
Let me always rejoice in my heart and celebrate
with others because of your marvelous work in my life.
Amen.

Before I formed thee

in the belly

I knew thee;

and before thou

camest forth

out of the womb

I sanctified thee.

Jeremiah 1:5

Picture This!

Some women, since girlhood, have kept a clear picture of what they've wanted to do in life, while others have struggled to find their place in life, with the picture changing as they respond to time and circumstance. God, however, has kept one picture and one picture only of you in His Heart since time began — the picture of a wonderful woman.

God's picture of you hasn't changed because, despite all the growing and changing you have done over the years, God remains unchanged. God is the almighty, all-powerful, and all-knowing God He always has been and always will be.

If you ever wonder how God sees you, just imagine Him holding a photo of you in a heart-shaped frame. This is how your God pictures you, and it's how many people whose lives you have touched picture you, too.

Lord God, you are a wonderful and gracious God!
Your picture of me as a wonderful woman
warms my heart and makes me desire
to follow you even more closely.
Amen.

I have learned,

in whatsoever state I am,

therewith to be content.

Philippians 4:11

Active
Contentment

Is contentment good? After all, aren't we supposed to get out of our comfort zone and go as far as we can go and do as much as we're able?

While setting God-pleasing goals for ourselves keeps us growing in exciting and productive ways, we must do so with an attitude of spiritual contentment with who we are and where we are today. The apostle Paul said he was content in whatever situation he found himself, yet he continued to actively spread the message of God's Love for all people. Paul was passionate about reaching even more communities and people with the good news, but he did so with a contented spirit.

Active contentment embraces the day with acceptance, with appreciation for the moment, and with willingness to move forward without fear. Yes, contentment is good!

Gracious Lord, fill my heart with your
spirit of contentment, and at the same time,
give me the courage and conviction it takes to go forward
with doing the things you would have me to do.
Amen.

Butter and honey

shall he eat,

that he may know to refuse the evil,

and choose the good.

Isaiah 7:15

A Matter of Choice

Some things in life we'd never choose for ourselves or our loved ones: sickness, accidents, emotional trauma, broken relationships. No, we'd never choose these things, but they come into our lives anyway. What we can choose, however, is how we react to them when they come.

We can choose to hunker down in denial, or accept a new reality with humility and grace. We can choose to turn inward in despair, or turn outward — and upward — to God. We can choose to lash out in anger, or allow others to help us through. Our attitude, our reaction to the problems we encounter, is something we can choose.

God chose you for Himself, and He has enabled you to choose the God-pleasing way to respond to life's inevitable problems, sufferings, and sorrows. It's a matter of choice.

Lord God, grant me the grace, faith, and strength to choose the good. Let my choices serve as an example for others, that they may be led to choose your way over any other. Amen.

Give ear, O LORD,

unto my prayer;

and attend to the voice

of my supplications.

Psalm 86:6

Let Us Pray

How do you pray? Some women recite the time-honored words of believers the world over, while others speak with God in the way they would talk to a friend. Some pray aloud and with other believers, while others pray silently in the sanctuary of the heart.

However you choose to pray, God listens. Of course He knows your needs and wants, and He knows what's happened to you today and what you think about it. Like a loving parent, however, God wants to hear you tell Him. He wants to have a conversation with you, a conversation where tears are shared, feelings are genuine, and laughter is frequent. In short, a conversation that is intimate.

In whatever way you're comfortable having such a conversation, that's the way God would have you pray to Him today and everyday.

God in heaven, receive my words
as I take all things to you in love and faith,
for this is the truest blessing of prayer between you
and each of your beloved children.
Amen.

Blessed be the God

and Father of our Lord Jesus Christ,

who hath blessed us

with all spiritual blessings

in heavenly places

in Christ.

Ephesians 1:3

You're Qualified

"God doesn't call the qualified, but He qualifies the called." The catchy phrase frequently seen on church bulletin boards expresses a profound truth. When God puts a task in front of us, He never wants to hear us say, "Sorry, I can't do this because I'm not qualified," because He knows we can't and we aren't. That's why, when God gives us a responsibility, we can rely on Him to give us the ability and the power to do it.

As a woman of God, you have God's assurance that you will be able to do all He asks of you from day to day. When your strength runs low, turn to Him for more. He has promised you will receive all you need.

Your God-given work always comes with God-given energy, strength, and power.

Lord God, give me everything I need
this day to do your will.
Grant me the faith and trust to turn to you
with all my needs.
Amen.

A bruised reed

shall he not break,

and the smoking flax

shall he not quench.

Isaiah 42:3

Renew

We get the message: repair, reuse, recycle! And though we may make every effort to fix what's broken instead of buying new, avoid disposables in favor of reusable items, and take our bottles, cans, and newspapers to the recycling center, there comes a time when something we own is just too broken to be of use to ourselves or anyone else. We throw it away.

God, however, never works that way with people, and He will never work that way with you. In God's economy, there's no such thing as a heart too broken or a spirit too damaged that He cannot renew it. There's no way you could become so wounded that your God could not make you whole again.

Renew is the only word you'll ever hear from God, and He promises to renew you every time you come to Him.

Heavenly Father, take me into your arms
and renew my spirit.
Grant me recovery from wounds of body and spirit,
and refresh me with the soothing balm of your love.
Amen.

Take care of him;

and whatsoever thou spendest more,

when I come again,

I will repay thee.

Luke 10:35

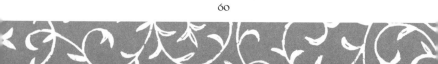

The Good Samaritan

In Jesus' story of the Good Samaritan, a man interrupts his journey to help someone who has been robbed and beaten and now lies in pain along the side of the road. Jesus told the story so we would have an example to follow in our own lives.

While Jesus cites someone in physical distress, we need not wait until we see a crime victim to practice Jesus' teaching. We are Good Samaritans when we stop what we're doing to comfort a child, mentor a co-worker, listen to a friend, help out in the family. We follow in the Good Samaritan's footsteps whenever we put aside what we had planned to do for the sake of what we need to do for someone in need.

God in His Goodness has given us the privilege of being Good Samaritans to one another. We can travel in confidence!

Savior Lord, thank you for the example of the Good Samaritan.
Let me be the one who's willing to stop
and help someone in need.
Amen.

Now then

we are ambassadors

for Christ.

2 Corinthians 5:20

Satisfaction Guaranteed

People are influenced by other people — advertisers know that, so they place people in their ads, people who are holding, using, and enjoying the product the advertisers want to sell.

In a similar way, God entrusts His message of love, forgiveness, and wholeness to people. When the Holy Spirit is at work in the hearts of God's people, they become God's ambassadors whose words and actions attract even more people, who themselves become ambassadors spreading God's message even further. There's nothing like the smile of a satisfied customer to attract the interest of other people!

Wonderful woman of God, the special things you do and say make you an ambassador of God's love, and perhaps that's why so many people are attracted to you!

Lord God, I humbly thank you
for using me to draw people to you.
Enable me to spread your message of love,
forgiveness, and wholeness
to all in need of your comfort and care.
Amen.

If any of you

lack wisdom,

let him ask of God,

that giveth

to all men liberally.

James 1:5

Sweet
Indulgence

If you have ever craved a luscious morsel of chocolate (and what woman hasn't?), then you know what it's like to be hungry for something. Whether what you crave is "good" or "bad" for you, you want to have it.

God encourages us to crave His wisdom with the same intensity we might crave a chocolate bar — or whatever our individual temptation might be. Only a craving for God's wisdom is a craving we can indulge without guilt, because it's a craving designed to draw us closer to God and enrich our relationship with others. There's another thing: God promises to let us have all the wisdom we ask for! When it comes to wisdom, we'll never hear God say, "Sorry, you've had enough!"

Ask and you will receive God's richest and sweetest blessing – His Wisdom. Indulge!

Lord God, I desire to receive the gift you so graciously promise to give — and give abundantly — to everyone who asks. Enable me to receive your wisdom and grow closer to you. Amen.

Hear me, O LORD;

for thy lovingkindness

is good: turn unto me

according to the multitude

of thy tender mercies.

Psalm 69:16

Glory Be!

Have you ever been surprised by the number of stars in the sky, or the perfection of a flower, or the trill of a songbird's melody? It's at times like these that the splendor of God's creative work comes front and center, but truly God's work is present in your familiar, everyday surroundings.

Through ordinary things, God reveals His Majesty and His Love. He doesn't stop first to determine if you have worked hard enough for the sun to rise, or recited a sufficient number of prayers for the seasons to turn. It happens because your compassionate God deals compassionately with people.

Just look around today and see for yourself evidence of His boundless love for people, then give Him thanks and praise for His unchanging and eternal love for you.

Creator God, you have made this world
to reflect your boundless love for your people.
Let the earth and everything in it remind me
to give you thanks and praise!
Amen.

Let us therefore

come boldly unto

the throne of grace,

that we may obtain mercy,

and find grace

to help in time of need.

Hebrews 4:16

Bold is Beautiful

Most of us know what it's like to speak to someone who's easily offended. We weigh every word, couching our true meaning in overly polite, even stilted, phrases. We watch the person carefully for signs of anger. We're definitely not comfortable!

While we want to come before God with the respect due Him, God also wants us to come to Him boldly even with those subjects that may be "uncomfortable". He doesn't want us to hold back our true feelings nor does He want us to measure our words to the point we are not honest with him.

He will not turn away from you in shock; in fact, He already knows every shadow of your mind and heart. He simply wants you to bring these unpleasant subjects to the forefront, with Him. A comfortable conversation with your God, even about difficult things, is not only possible, it's welcome, and it's beautiful.

Almighty God, in your goodness you invite the words
and feelings of your people.
Grant me confidence in your love for me
so that I may always come before you
with honesty, boldness, and joy.
Amen.

If thine enemy be hungry,

give him bread to eat;

and if he be thirsty,

give him water to drink:

for thou shalt heap

coals of fire upon his head.

Proverbs 25:21–22

Coals of Fire

The writer of the book of Proverbs has an imaginative way of treating enemies. Forgive them, he advises, and you will heap coals of fire on his head! While we may smile to picture our enemies walking around with singed hair, God has a real-world purpose in these words.

When you make no attempt to get even with someone who has hurt you, your behavior stands out, because it's completely unexpected. People are watching, and when they don't see anger or retaliation on your part, they take notice — and so does the person who has hurt you. When you treat him or her with kindness and compassion, the heat of embarrassment may well feel like burning coals.

You have set the stage for the person to ask forgiveness and for yourself to offer it. This is how God's work gets done in the real world.

Lord of love, as you forgive me, enable me by the power of your
spirit to forgive others. Let me never try to get even,
but give forgiveness, so they may experience
your mercy and grace.
Amen.

So then because thou art lukewarm,

and neither cold nor hot,

I will spew thee out of my mouth.

Revelation 3:16

Yes

"Well, yes and no." We use this phrase when asked a question that calls for a complicated explanation. We want the person we are speaking with to listen to our complete answer and not reach a simple, but false, conclusion.

When it comes to the matter of commitment to God, however, we're compelled to give a straight "yes" or "no" answer. God accepts no in-between, because He wants each one of us to know clearly in our own mind whether or not we're willing to follow Him. If we think we can live in some gray area outside of "yes" or "no," we are fooling ourselves.

Your gracious God invites you to say "yes" to Him each day, because He says "yes" to you each hour, each minute of your life.

Lord, your "yes" to me enables me to say "yes" to you,
and it is in this "yes" that I give thanks
and praise to you now and forever.
Amen.

I have lived

in all good conscience

before God

until this day.

Acts 23:1

Living the Authentic Life

All too often we witness the sad spectacle of someone compelled to give up a thriving ministry or the privilege of public office because his or her behavior fell far short of the individual's stated beliefs.

We say we're Christian, but human frailty guarantees there will be slip-ups along the way, and there will be times we will not live up to God's will and rules. God will not show contempt for us, nor will He insist we leave Him. He will continue to love us, and He has promised forgiveness when we come to Him with a repentant heart.

Nothing you have ever done or could do will change God's mind about you belonging to Him, about you talking about Him to others, about you taking His Love into the world. He is your God, and you are His child forever.

Heavenly Father, guide me in my life, and with the power of your spirit, enable me to bring my faith and my life together as one in word and action.
Amen.

Now therefore ye are no more

strangers and foreigners,

but fellowcitizens with the saints,

and of the household

of God.

Ephesians 2:19

All in Your Family

In God's household, no one's a stranger. Everyone who comes to God is received by God as a beloved daughter or son, and as a member of His family.

Ideally, Christians together reflect the relationship they share with God as their Father, but unfortunately, not every community of Christians measures up. Why? Because human frailty follows them into the house of God. When the church door opens, weakness walks in. For this reason, we cannot leave God's love and forgiveness outside the church door, but we must bring it inside and practice it in our conversations, committee meetings, and worship with and among our fellow Christians.

God invites you to enter His household of faith, and rejoice with your sisters and brothers, all children of your Heavenly Father.

Father in heaven, I thank you for the presence of other believers
in my life. Together, let us work to your glory,
love each other, and worship you in unity.
Amen.

Except the LORD

build the house,

they labour in vain

that build it.

Psalm 127:1

The Builder

You probably would not need to look far to find someone whose plans have gone awry. Maybe it's even happened to you: despite all the reasonable precautions you took and all the thoughtful preparation you gave, and all the effort you put into it, things just didn't work out.

While human-made plans may fail for any number of reasons — some beyond our control — God's plans have been in place since before the world began, and they're still in place today. The sun, moon, and stars are still in the heavens, and the seasons still mark the years. Children are born and grow to maturity, and people still hear the voice of God calling them through the ordinary events of life.

You can rely on God being there for you. He always has been, and He always will be.

Lord God, build in me a living and lively faith
that will withstand all that happens to me in my life.
If all else crumbles, your love will endure!
Amen.

And now these three remain:

faith, hope and love.

But the greatest of these

is love.

1 Corinthians 13:13 NIV

Greatest
of These

The greatest of these is love! Though we often hear these familiar words read during wedding ceremonies, these same words apply in our everyday lives and in all our relationships. In its original meaning, the word translated as love refers to brotherly love, to an over-arching attitude of respect, compassion, and tolerance toward our family, friends, co-workers, and the people we associate with in the normal course of our day. This overall attitude, this central perspective, is one of love for others, the greatest (and most enduring) of all gifts, qualities, and virtues.

God enables you to approach people with an attitude of love, a love that emanates from love-based thoughts, words, and actions. In God's Spirit, all your relationships are defined by love.

God of love, fill my heart with the kind of love
that reaches out to others with your kindness, compassion,
caring, and ever-enduring love.
Amen.

And Jesus answering said,

Were there not ten cleansed?

but where are the nine?

Luke 17:17

One in Ten

When Jesus healed ten lepers of their debilitating disease, only one man came back to thank Jesus for what He had done. Only one!

Most of us would get tired of giving gifts to someone who rarely took the time to send a thank-you note or call and tell us how much the gift was enjoyed. In all probability, we would remove that person's name from our gift list. God is different, however. Whether or not anyone thanks Him for the blessings received from His generous hand each day, God continues to shower the world with His Blessings.

Give thanks, beloved woman of God, that you know to whom to give thanks! Rejoice that you are the one in ten who remembers to say thank you to the source of all your gifts and blessings.

Lord God, thank you for all the gifts
and blessings I receive from you each day.
Let me never take your goodness
and generosity for granted.
Amen.

Now there are

diversities of gifts,

but the same Spirit.

1 Corinthians 12:4

Opportunity for All

Throughout the Bible, you read accounts of women who have been community leaders, lay ministers, teachers, tailors, travelers, homemakers, merchants, and fundraisers. It's clear, God is an equal opportunity employer!

Today, God uses the various gifts, skills, and talents of women for the benefit of family, friends, and community, and there's no one — woman or man — God cannot and will not put to work in some way. Though not everyone will be doing the same thing, no one's work is expendable or less significant in God's eyes than anyone else's.

What are the specific gifts, talents, abilities, and interests God has given to you? Use each one to the fullest, for in this you will find your greatest opportunity, your greatest joy.

Lord God, thank you for the gifts and abilities you have given to me. Keep me focused on what I can do for the good of those around me.
Amen.

And he turned him

unto his disciples,

and said privately,

Blessed are the eyes

which see the things

that ye see.

Luke 10:23

20/20 *Vision*

Most of us notice our eyesight declining as we age, and some of us have been partially or completely blind for many years. The condition of our physical eyes, while significant to the way we perceive the things of the world, is insignificant when it comes to the way we perceive the things of the spirit.

God's Spirit dwells in the heart, and it is through the workings of God's Spirit that we receive our spiritual eyesight. God's Spirit cures our spiritual blindness, sharpens our spiritual vision, and deepens our understanding of spiritual matters. Our spiritual eyes begin to see our great God at work in our lives and in the world.

Blessed are you, for you see God with the eyes of your spirit. Rejoice, because unlike physical eyesight, spiritual eyesight just keeps getting sharper!

God, come into my heart and enable me
to see you better as I draw closer to you
in faith and in love.
Amen.

He hath shewed thee,

O man, what is good;

and what doth

the LORD require of thee,

but to do justly,

and to love mercy,

and to walk humbly

with thy God?

Micah 6:8

Join Him

Colleges and universities require admittance tests, country clubs ask for membership dues, and homeowners' associations dictate what you can and cannot build on your property. To join any number of organizations, there is money to pay and there are rules to follow!

God's requirements are different. They're simple, fee-free, and accessible to all. Anyone and everyone can choose to do the right thing, to say the kind word. Anyone and everyone can opt for compassion and caring, and anyone and everyone, enabled by God's Spirit, can leave the self behind, step alongside God, and walk with Him in humility and peace.

If you ever feel burdened by requirements, turn to the God who invites you to join Him just as you are. There's nothing you need to do first or pay up-front. It's truly a join as-you-are affair.

*Lord, I'm humbled and grateful
that you reach out to embrace me just as I am.
Remove the burden of man-made requirements
from me so I may walk with you.
Amen.*

And it shall come to pass,

that before they call,

I will answer;

and while they are

yet speaking,

I will hear.

Isaiah 65:24

Listen Up

Among some people, it's hard to get a word in edgewise, and when you finally do, you wonder whether or not anyone has heard you. When you pray, however, you have no such worries.

God promises you many times throughout the Bible that He is willing and able to listen to you when you pray — in fact, He's listening before you ever start to speak! Speak at length, and never feel hurried. God isn't checking His watch or cell phone for the time. And most importantly, know that your words matter! When you're finished, take a tip from what God has just done for you: listen!

The willingness and the patience to listen to others is a blessing you can shower on those who speak to you today.

Lord God, grant me confidence that you hear
my prayers and you answer them.
Enable me to do for others
what you so graciously do for me — let me listen!
Amen.

And the Lord

direct your hearts

into the love of God.

2 Thessalonians 3:5

The Right Direction

On the road, men hate to ask directions, at least according to jokes and humorous anecdotes. By contrast, women have no problem stopping and asking for directions when the road signs aren't leading to where they want to go.

It may be easy and natural, then, for us to ask and receive spiritual directions from God when we realize we're not where we want to be in spirit, heart, and mind. When the landscape around us becomes frightening and unfamiliar, we will turn to God for help and guidance. When we find ourselves far from God's peace, we have no problem asking God if we're going in the right direction.

God is available at any time to give directions and put you once again on the path with and toward Him. All you need to do is ask.

Heavenly Father, keep me always willing to ask for your guidance,
your directions. Grant me a heart willing and able
to follow your commandments.
Amen.

I will abundantly bless

her provision:

I will satisfy her poor

with bread.

Psalm 132:15

Riches to Spare

Few of us are so wealthy that we don't notice when the price of food, utilities, and fuel escalates. At the same time, there are many women of faith who are so rich in faith and love that they don't notice that they're doing more and more for others!

Women of faith who begin serving others find they are asked time and again to serve, and they are happy to do it. Their time is no more abundant than anyone else's, but their God-given and Spirit-fed faith is. The more these busy women serve, the more faith God pours into their hearts, so their service is given out of abundance! They probably don't even notice how much they do.

The beauty of true wealth is this: the more you give, the richer you become!

Lord God, let me never hold back,
but step forward in generous service to others
out of the abundance of the faith and love
you have put into my heart.
Amen.

Be still, and know

that I am God.

Psalm 46:10

Heart's Peace

For some women, a quiet time during the day is an impossible dream. Time out to be alone and meditate just isn't going to happen on a regular basis, and they know it.

If you find yourself without the luxury of quiet time alone each day, remember there's still a peaceful and quiet place you can go to worship and honor God — inside the sanctuary of your own heart. There you can reach out to God with your words and feelings, your joys and your sorrows. In your heart, you can give God the quiet space He needs to offer you His comfort and care, and in your heart you can lean on His presence and protection.

When quiet time just isn't going to happen on the outside, take the quiet inside. God is there, waiting for you.

God of peace, I long for serenity of spirit
and quiet time with you.
Come inside the sanctuary of my heart,
and let me dwell in your peace.
Amen.

Let your light so shine

before men,

that they may see

your good works,

and glorify your Father

which is in heaven.

Matthew 5:16

Let Your Light Shine

Have you ever walked at night down a dark street and then spotted a bright, shining street light ahead? It's a welcome sight and a good feeling to move out of the shadows and into the security and safety of light!

In a world darkened by self–interest and selfishness, the self–sacrificing things faithful women do are like shining lights. In the shadow of gossip, slander, and back–biting, the kind and caring things faithful women say offer safety and warmth to others. In life's journey often embittered by ignorance, the compassion of God's faithful women shines like the warmth of the sun on grieving souls.

Never give up letting your light shine! You never know when someone is in desperate need of hope, of illumination.

Lord God, may all I do be done to your glory.
Let those who are touched by the light
of things I do and say recognize you.
Amen.

All that the Father

giveth me

shall come to me;

and him that cometh to me

I will in no wise cast out.

John 6:37

Room for More

"The door is always open for you!" That's what a family member or a good friend might say to you, and it's the same thing God declares to you, His precious child.

No woman needs to fear that God's door will be slammed in her face because of some real or perceived fault she finds in herself, or that she will be left standing on the porch wringing her hands while she watches others invited in to the party. The God who opens his door to all is the same God who loves you with intensity beyond earthly imagination, and there's no way He's going to leave you standing around outside!

Let others know what you know – God's door is always open, and there's always room for one more!

Heavenly Father, you bless my life
with the assurance of your acceptance and love.
Enable me to tell others of your gracious
and unchanging invitation!
Amen.

I thank my God

upon every remembrance

of you.

Philippians 1:3

Fond Remembrance

There are people who have come into our lives that we love to remember. When we think of these special people, we recall once more the sound of their voice, their favorite sayings, the look they give that always warms the heart.

Our loved ones — whether near or far, friends or family, co-workers or merely acquaintances we have met along the path of life — are blessings from the hand of God. They contribute love and laughter, care and companionship, and a wealth of memories and the expectation of more good times to come. Without them, life would be a sad and lonely journey!

As you give thanks to God for your loved ones, your friends, the people you meet, know that they give thanks to God for you.

Dear Lord, I thank you for those I name,
those people who have added and continue to add
so much love and joy to my life.
Amen.

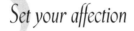

Set your affection

on things above,

not on things

on the earth.

Colossians 3:2

Reach Up

Some women of past eras were cautioned by their mothers not to aim too high. These well-meaning mothers, aware of the limits placed on women's achievement at the time, did not want to see their daughters hurt. But for all believers of all eras, God offers different advice. He says, "Reach high! Don't be satisfied with earthly goals! Reach higher than earth itself!"

God expects all of us to use the skills and talents He has given us to their fullest, but He doesn't expect us to stop there. God puts in front of us much higher things, and on these things, these spiritual things, He wants us to set our heart.

Love, joy, peace, faith, goodness — these are the higher things, and don't be afraid to reach for them!

God in heaven, let me not be afraid
to reach up for those things above,
for these are the things that will never pass away,
but last forever.
Amen.

Humble yourselves therefore

under the mighty hand of God,

that he may exalt you

in due time:

casting all your care upon him;

for he careth for you.

1 Peter 5:6–7

Care and Caring

At sometime in their lives, most women find themselves caring for someone. It might be caring for young children, caring for a stricken spouse, caring for a sick friend, or caring for an elderly parent. As these women well know, the day–to–day responsibilities of a caregiver can become burdensome.

While friends and family members may be able to offer needed support and help, God offers far more. To all caregivers and to anyone going through a rough time, God provides assurance that He will use their specific situation as a means to lift them up closer to Him in faith and trust. And He provides immediate relief, too. "Caregivers, give all your cares to me," God says, "and give them to me right now."

When you give care to others, remember to give all your cares to God.

Dear Lord, your care for me touches
my heart and gives me strength to care for others.
Let me never lose my love for you
and ever trust you in all things.
Amen.

Fear not, little flock;

for it is your Father's

good pleasure

to give you

the kingdom.

Luke 12:32

Afraid No Longer

"Don't be afraid," we tell ourselves, but our words fail to take away our true feelings. Depending on our situation, we either back away in fear or forge ahead with our stomach in knots. But when God says, "Don't be afraid," His words come weighted with the power to banish our fear and give us the courage we need to go forward.

God, who spoke and the world came into being, speaks with authority. Things happen because of His words! His words convey the truth and establish the truth. In the Bible, God's commandments, plans, and promises are woven tightly together like the fibers of a strong net to bring us the security of His firm, unchangeable, and unchanging word.

The next time you're frightened, take courage, because the words "Don't be afraid" aren't your words, but God's.

Lord God, when I'm frightened,
remind me of your words and promises.
Be with me, Lord, and I will not be afraid.
Amen.

And he said,

Who art thou, Lord?

And the Lord said,

I am Jesus

whom thou persecutest.

Acts 9:5

Living Proof

By way of a blinding light and a commanding voice, God transformed Saul, the persecutor, to Paul, the missionary. While God seldom employs such dramatic means to change people, He still has the power to do so.

The Holy Spirit works in our hearts to turn us toward God's will and His Word. God's Holy Spirit gives, nurtures, and strengthens the seed of faith within us, whether this seed has been growing for years, or it has only begun to sprout. We have living proof of God's transforming work when we make time for prayer and worship, when we perceive and treat others as God's beloved people, when we more faithfully take on the mind and heart of God.

Though God may not have struck you down to get your attention, God's Spirit is at work in you. You're living proof!

Lord God, let your Holy Spirit live within me,
day by day transforming my heart
to reflect your goodness and love.
Amen.

O keep my soul,

and deliver me:

let me not be ashamed;

for I put my trust in thee.

Psalm 25:20

No Shame in Trying

Is it your dream to learn a new skill, a new sport, a new craft? Begin a new career? Embrace a long-time passion? If you hesitate to follow your dream because you want to avoid the possibilty of failure, you're in good company. The Psalmist felt the same way!

Anxiety over the shame of failure all too frequently convinces us not to try in the first place. We come up with all sorts of excuses, but fundamentally, we're afraid of facing disappointment and, perhaps even more, we fear disappointing those we love. That's a shame! When we have a God-given and God-pleasing dream or ambition, our God says, "Go for it!"

God has enriched your life with the blessing of dreams, ambitions, and aspirations. The real shame lies in being afraid to start.

Dear God, according to your will, grant me the opportunity,
resources, and courage I need to follow the dreams
and passions of my heart.
Amen.

The LORD

hath made bare his holy arm

in the eyes of all the nations;

and all the ends of the earth

shall see the salvation

of our God.

Isaiah 52:10

See and Believe

"Seeing is believing," the familiar maxim declares, but there's an exception when it comes to God's presence and His creative powers. Not everyone who sees the forests and hills, the meadows and streams, the oceans and skies, believes God made them. Not everyone who receives healing, feels comforted, or who experiences love, believes that God has anything to do with it. Seeing isn't necessarily believing!

What about you? Do you see God in His glorious handiwork? How much in your life convinces you that God, your God, is worthy of your full trust, your heartfelt praise, your firm belief? No doubt, your list could stretch through eternity! You have been blessed with seeing eyes.

Let your words and actions show others the goodness of your God. Help them see and believe.

Creator God, thank you for the ways
you have made yourself known in my life.
Grant me the privilege of bringing others
to see you, know you, and believe in you.
Amen.

Fight the good fight

of the faith,

lay hold

on eternal life.

1 Timothy 6:12

Speak Up

Most of us will go out of our way to avoid uncomfortable confrontations and heated battles. When we find ourselves in the middle of a shouting match, we're likely to keep ourselves as quiet and as inconspicuous as possible.

When it comes to matters of faith, however, we should be compelled to stand up for what we believe and for the spiritual truths God has put into our hearts. If we don't speak up, our silence could be perceived as uncertainty, or as agreement with opinions we know, by conviction and experience, fly in the face of God's clearly stated word. If we don't speak, how can they hear the truth?

When you speak up for your faith, you may or may not be successful in convincing others. But that is not what God asks you to do. He asks only that you speak up.

Dear Lord, replace my fear with the courage
to tell the truth in love,
to speak up for my faith
and my relationship with you.
Amen.

Give me

neither poverty

nor riches;

feed me with food

convenient for me.

Proverbs 30:8

Enough

In tough economic times, there is more focused attention on the previously reviled principles of thrift and moderation. The wisest among us have long known that more is rarely necessary nor better, and others among us have learned the lesson for themselves.

In most cases, more is simply too much — too much to maintain, too much to store, too much to pay for. In a tight economy, almost all of us practice examining our budgets, asking what in life we really value and whether or not what we might want at the moment is something we really need and can pay for.

If you wonder what good news could come out of economic bad news, it's this: a return to a godly perspective on wants and needs, and the God-given wisdom to buy accordingly.

Dear God, infuse my heart with
a spirit of moderation so I may use,
enjoy, and appreciate the material things
I'm privileged to possess.
Amen.

But those who suffer

he delivers in their suffering;

he speaks to them

in their affliction.

Job 36:15 NIV

Firm Faith

Some people mistakenly believe that being firm in their faith means never having doubts. Nothing could be further from the facts! As long as we're living this side of heaven, our faith will be spotted with doubts and pocked with question marks.

Our strong faith holds firmly to God's promises, despite the times we wonder about God's purposes and the times we question what God says and His ways with people. The difference between believers and unbelievers is this: unbelievers use their doubts and questions as excuses not to believe, while believers take their doubts and questions directly to God.

Woman of God, when you are disturbed by doubts about God's promises and bothered by questions about God's way with you and those you love, talk to God. He has promised to speak with you in your doubts, in your questions.

Almighty God, let my doubts and my questions
come before you. Strengthen my trust in your promises
and keep my faith firmly in your word.
Amen.

For what shall

it profit a man,

if he shall gain

the whole world,

and lose his own soul?

Mark 8:36

Mature Choices

As we mature, we find ourselves able to make mature choices. Going along with the crowd lessens in importance to embracing the choices that are right for us and the life we want for ourselves.

Spiritual maturity works in much the same way. As we grow closer to God and mature in spirit, we begin to make spiritually mature choices. We realize that many beliefs and values held by the world might fill our days with pleasure now, and even bring us popularity, but will bring us emptiness, if not devastation, later. Enabled by God's Spirit at work in us, we opt for the spiritually mature choice.

The temptation to fit in, to go along with the crowd, is strong, but God's power at work in the spiritually mature is even stronger.

God of all eternity,
feed me with your wisdom so that in all my choices,
I will grow closer to you in heart and mind.
Amen.

Ye shall be

my people,

and I will be

your God.

Ezekiel 36:28

Certain and Sure

When we face uncertain times, we need only look back in history to realize that people throughout the ages have lived in uncertain times also. In no day since time began has anyone been promised a problem-free life!

All God's people, however, have been promised a God-filled life, a life in relationship with Almighty God who has taken it upon Himself to reach out to those who so often stumble, stray, and prefer their own way. Since time began, God has been calling and communicating with people for the purpose of revealing Himself to them, of illuminating for them His Work in their lives, and of telling them about His Plan for their salvation.

Remember, in uncertain times, one thing remains certain and sure, and that's God's unconditional love for you.

Almighty God, take me by the hand
in uncertain times and fill my heart with the certainty
of your power, presence, and promises.
Amen.

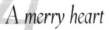

A merry heart

doeth good

like a medicine.

Proverbs 17:22

Ha, ha, ha!

"An apple a day keeps the doctor away," and the same case could be made for a daily dose of laughter. Laughter lifts us up and makes us feel good in body and soul!

Wholesome, healthy laughter makes others feel good, too. Have you ever noticed how humor has a way of drawing people together? There are few better ways to say "I understand you, I'm with you" than to hear the music of another person's laughter, let loose, and laugh right along. Very often, a light-hearted moment of shared laughter is the beginning of a close and lifelong friendship.

When happiness lifts your spirit, don't be afraid to laugh out loud, because laughter is catching — it lifts the spirits of everyone around you!

Lord God, you have blessed me with the gift of laughter.
Grant me the happiness of using it
to lift my heart and the hearts of others.
Amen.

But seek ye first

the kingdom of God,

and his righteousness;

and all these things

shall be added

unto you.

Matthew 6:33

Keep Pace

If you were to name the most urgent to-do in front of you today, would you be able to keep it to only one thing? Like many women, you may be hard pressed to say which to-do takes top priority in a list of important, necessary, and must-do-now items!

Our own expectations and the urgencies of others can effectively keep us darting from one thing to another in a daily race against time to get things done. We hate the pace, but we see no other option, that is, unless we're willing to give God's option a try. God says, "Put me first in mind and heart."

When you make God and Him alone, your top priority, you will be able to do everything else at a doable, peaceable, and human pace.

God of eternity, help me arrange my days,
my time, and my priorities
with you as number one in time,
commitment, and loyalty.
Amen.

He asked his disciples,

saying unto them,

Whom do men say

that I am?

Mark 8:27

Who Am I?

You've no doubt heard people talk about their perception of God. For some, God is a grandfatherly figure sitting in heaven, indulgently spoiling His earthly children. For others, God is a stern judge keeping strict record of each individual's pluses and minuses.

While God certainly richly blesses us and surely sees us as we are, He is much more. In the Bible, God reveals Himself as creator, savior, and comforter. As creator, God our father made the world and gave us life. As savior, God in Jesus brought forgiveness and salvation to us and showed us God's compassion and love. As comforter, God the Holy Spirit continues to nurture and strengthen the bonds between God and His earthly children.

How would you answer if God were to ask you, "Whom do you say that I am?"

Lord God, grant me the gift of knowing you
as you have revealed yourself in the Bible.
Keep my thoughts of you grounded in
and faithful to your word.
Amen.

But the water

that I shall give him

shall be in him

a well of water

springing up

into everlasting life.

John 4:14

Fresh Water

Fresh water is essential to human life, and perhaps that's why Jesus chose cool, clear water drawn from a well to illustrate His message and work of salvation. As our physical life depends on a constant supply of fresh water, so our spiritual life depends on the clear word of God drawn daily to nourish and refresh us.

As we read and meditate on Scripture each day, we begin to discover fresh and timely applications of God's word. A verse we may have glossed over in the past now shimmers to life and explodes with meaning, or a parable we've heard many times now bursts with relevance to something we're going through right now.

Drink, and drink deeply and drink daily, from the waters of God's living word to you.

*God of the Bible, thank you for holding out
to me the living water of your word.
Let me come to you daily to renew
and refresh myself in your love.
Amen.*

But our

citizenship

is in heaven.

Philippians 3:20 NIV

We Belong

We're proud citizens of our country, and at the same time we're proud citizens of heaven.

As our country provides us with certain freedoms, so does heaven. To our country and to heaven, we have the freedom to be loyal or disloyal, supportive or destructive, productive or unproductive. We can sing our country's, or heaven's, praises or speak out against it. We're free to obey or disobey its laws, enhance or smear its reputation among others, and we're even free to choose citizenship elsewhere, if we like.

When God brought you into heavenly citizenship, He also gave you the freedom to choose how your citizenship will be lived on earth and its meaning in your life. Take a few moments to tell God what your heavenly citizenship means to you.

Gracious God, thank you for making me
a citizen of my country and of heaven.
Grant me the grace to treat both citizenships with love,
respect, and gratitude.
Amen.

Behold, as the eyes

of servants look unto the hand

of their masters,

and as the eyes of a maiden

unto the hand of her mistress;

so our eyes

wait upon the LORD

our God.

Psalm 123:2

Sinners and Saints

We're constantly learning from others. We learn what to avoid from the mistakes of others, and we learn how to proceed in our own lives from the successes of others.

By meditating on the lives of the men and women of the Bible, we learn even more. We learn that even the heroes and heroines of the Bible were sinners and saints, just as we are. Biblical people of God made mistakes, had weaknesses, suffered loss, and even wavered in faith at times. But they also obeyed God's commandments, hung onto His Promises, stood up to persecution, and encouraged others in the faith.

If you see your own life reflected in the lives of Biblical men and women, don't be surprised. The Bible is, after all, a place God's people go to learn from God's people.

Heavenly Father, I give thanks for the example
set by the men and women of the Bible.
Help me learn from them and walk in the way of the truth.
Amen.

Finally,

be ye all of one mind,

having compassion

one of another,

love as brethren.

1 Peter 3:8

Helping Hands

Occasionally, all of us need help, even the most independent among us. But for women accustomed to being the one people rely on to be there in times of need, it's especially difficult to recognize their own need for help, ask another person to do something for them, and accept the efforts of others gladly and graciously.

While a popular saying claims that it's better to give rather than to receive, God would have us live as both giver and receiver. Often we're very good at giving of ourselves, our time, and our heart to those in need, but God wants us to be good at receiving the selfless gifts of others, as well.

Are you able to offer others the blessing and the privilege of helping you? The next time you need it, don't hesitate to ask — and receive.

Lord God, just as you have given me
the privilege of giving help to others,
grant me the generosity of spirit
to graciously receive help in times of need.
Amen.

And whatsoever ye do

in word or deed,

do all in the name

of the Lord Jesus.

Colossians 3:17

What's in a Name?

When we have a specific goal in mind, our actions work to achieve our goal. We're likely to shake off any activities that would lessen our chances of reaching our goal, regarding them as time- and energy-wasters. Once we have a specific goal, everything we do, we do in the name of that goal.

The goal of living a more spiritual life works the same way. Activities that don't work to achieve the spiritual life, that don't add to our understanding of God and fail to benefit others, we simply stop doing. These things no longer interest us and we avoid wasting our time and energy on them. We would much rather be spending our time and resources on God-pleasing, productive, and worthwhile pursuits.

Let everything you do be done in the name of your Lord.

Dear Lord, let the goal of my life
be to know you better and serve you by serving others.
Let all I do be done in your name!
Amen.

Beloved, follow not

that which is evil,

but that which is good.

He that doeth good

is of God:

but he that doeth evil

hath not seen God.

3 John 1:11

A Matter of Recognition

The faces of people we haven't seen in years gradually fade from our memory. If we meet them again, it might take us a few seconds to recognize them and put a name to their face.

After we have been away from hearing, reading, and meditating on God's word, little by little we forget what God looks like in our lives. We let His daily blessings slip by us without notice, and we fail to see His loving touch in the kindness, compassion, and friendship of others. Even more, we lose the ability to recognize God's face in our godly actions, replacing His features with our own reflection.

Beloved woman of God, so many others see God's face in the things you do and say. Never give up the privilege of recognizing Him, too!

Lord, let me ever treasure the time I spend in your presence,
that the beauty of your face may always
remain familiar to my heart.
Amen.

The LORD bless thee,
and keep thee:
The LORD make his face
shine upon thee,
and be gracious unto thee:
The LORD lift up
his countenance upon thee,
and give thee peace.

Numbers 6:24-26